Hare

HUGH DUNKERLEY

Published by Cinnamon Press
Meirion House
Glan yr afon
Tanygrisiau
Blaenau Ffestiniog
Gwynedd
LL41 3SU
www.cinnamonpress.com

Designed and typeset in Palatino by Cinnamon Press. Cover design by Mike Fortune-Wood from original artwork 'European Hare Running' by Ambrogio Coralloni
The epigraph is from Annie Dillard, *Pilgrim at Tinker Creek*. Picador, 1976. Used with kind permission.

Printed in Poland.

Cinnamon Press is represented in the UK by Inpress Ltd www.inpressbooks.co.uk and in Wales by the Welsh Books Council www.cllc.org.uk.

Acknowledgements

I would like to thank the editors of the following magazines and anthologies in which some of these poems first appeared: *Orbis, Last Steps* (Giant Steps), *BBC Wildlife Magazine, The Fiddlehead* (Canada), *ISLE* (USA), *Irish Pages, Staple, Succour, The London Magazine, Hand Luggage* (Open Poetry) *The Gregory Poems 1991-1993* (Sinclair Stevenson), *Writing on Water* (MIT), *Oxford Poets 2007* (Carcanet), *Poetry South* and *The Joy Magazine.* A number of poems were originally published in two pamphlet collections, *Walking to the Fire Tower* (Redbeck Press, 1997) and *Fast* (Pighog Press, 2007). I would also like to thank the administrators of Hawthornden Castle for awarding me a Hawthornden Fellowship, the Banff Centre for the Arts, where I was fortunate to be a Leighton Fellow, and the Arts Council of England for a grant to aid the completion of this collection. I am particularly grateful to the following for their feedback and encouragement: Bethan Roberts, Dave Swann, Naomi Foyle, Lorna Thorpe, Kai Merriot, Stephanie Norgate, John Davies, Alison MacLeod, Karen Stevens, David Craig, Christopher North, Vicki Feaver, Maggie Sawkins, Robert Hamberger, Stuart Pickford, George Marsh, Elaine Crinnion, Bernard McDonagh, Andrew Sant, Mark Doty and Penelope Shuttle.

Contents

We wake, if we ever wake at all, to mystery, rumours of death, beauty, violence...

Annie Dillard

Hare

for Bethan

In the Darkroom

How to Walk on a Knife Edge

First, remember that this may hurt,
your feet may bleed
because it must be done in bare feet;
shoes are no good,
in fact you must be completely naked.
Then, placing one foot on the cold steel,
press down until you can feel
the knife's edge along the whole of your sole.
Quickly transfer your weight to the other foot.
You must keep moving;
any hesitation at this stage could be fatal.
Halfway along there is always the temptation
to look back and see how far you've travelled.
Resist. Keep your eye instead
on the next millimetre of metal
and then the next and the next.
If you keep your head
you may make it to the other side
without flaying your feet to ribbons.
Then you can look back
and wonder how you managed for so long
to stay upright on that unremitting tightrope.

Rock Drill

after Epstein

The whole thing seems to be vibrating,
the insect god on his tripod,
the head a mask of anguish.

Between his legs
the huge drill yammers away
at the absent rock

or is it a weapon,
is he a gunner in armour
mowing down a notional enemy?

An emaciated jockey,
he seems to grow
out of the machinery

because there's nowhere it stops
and he begins,
just the same steel

black as a beetle's carapace
from the stanchion legs
to the jutting girder of his neck.

Between armoured ribs,
his progeny hunkers down
ticking like a bomb.

Even his head's becoming something else,
the forehead a helmet,
the long snout a visor,

the eyes peeking out of their slots
like ball bearings.
Oil, he seems to say, *bit, swivel,*

ammunition.
The world is there:
it must be remade.

Early Warning

Suddenly the bees deserted the air,
the hives fell silent
and the garden filled with their absence.

Meanwhile the numb flowers
went on offering up their sweet surfeit
to nothing and to no one

and he scoured the skies
for some dark unseen threat.
Later, as he was planting

the first of the new potatoes,
the rain came, running in rivulets
down his back, soaking his shoes,

drumming on the hives like hail.
That evening, on the news, he heard
about the stricken reactor,

thought of the potatoes in their darkness
ticking with danger,
of his own wet skin, how by morning

the bees would be swarming
at the hive exits,
yearning for nectar.

Astronaut

I turned them off, the voices,
and hung in my metal shelter,
effortlessly in nothingness.

Underneath me was the planet,
a deep blue fleeced with tiny clouds,
and on the horizon, Africa's glowing brownness.

I felt the agony of separation,
how the sun blazed, intolerable
without the filter of atmosphere,

how the moon loomed, a pitted wreck,
failed and lifeless,
and the silence dinned.

Then they pulled me back
through the incandescence of re-entry.

Child

You were sleeping when they found you,
curled in a ditch, long summer grasses
bending down to brush your senseless face.
You never heard the clatter of the circling helicopter,
never noticed the men and women
in dazzling overalls combing the fields,
the battery of bristling cameras
waiting for you at the end of the lane.
You were silent when they asked
about the men who'd taken you,
what they'd done to you
with hands, threats, caresses,
how for weeks the grasses had gradually
closed out the light until you were finally
cocooned in a green darkness.
You never woke when they lifted you,
naked, from your hiding place
and carried you away,
some skin cells, a few stray hairs,
floating down onto the broken ground,
already finding their way
in the long slow sift of matter.

Fast

For days you must have lived on air,
the exaltation of hunger,
your stomach shrinking to a knot

until you couldn't feel anything,
not even the cold that had wracked you
through your thin sleeping bag, night and day.

In the tent crumpled biscuits, chocolate,
a half-opened tin of condensed milk
were scattered out of reach, the remnants

of a rite you'd long forgotten.
In the granite light the mountains wavered
while at night the stars rustled, tugging

at you with their tiny gravities.
You must have thought you were close then,
the chrysalis perhaps of something unimaginable.

When the last agonies came, the muscles,
the organs, consuming themselves in a final blaze,
what a purification it must have seemed.

The Guardians of the Water

for Chris

They came in the middle of the night
—three old men he'd seen at the bar
and thought nothing of—
banging on the big wooden door,
asking for the señora,
not even meeting his eye.

His wife, wrapped in her dressing gown,
still tidying her hair with one hand,
spoke rapidly in Spanish,
and led them down to the kitchen.

Standing by the sink, he felt excluded,
just as he'd done at that bullfight,
the crowd seething round him,
his head aching from the heat,
the trembling bull, bloodied and exhausted,
collapsing in the dirt.

Then one of the old men produced a sledgehammer
—from where he couldn't imagine—
and with a soft thud
knocked a hole in the back wall.

In the semi-darkness he could hardly make them out,
the three of them
crouched by the white-edged hole,
muttering something about drought,
the old Arab water course
that used to run below the house.

They said little as they left,
just grunted to his wife and were gone.
He wanted to know who was going to pay for the plaster,
but his wife shrugged, said she was sleepy
and that she was going back to bed.

The next day, walking in the garden,
he was sure he could hear the sound of running water,
detect its clear metallic tang—
like the smell of an English summer day after rain—
among the hot scents of rosemary and thyme.

Cross-Border

Armagh, 1993

It was late when you finally left
and the cold air and the silence
and the land black under
a sky littered with stars
made you pause,
catch your breath.
You felt the fog of the wine lifting,
knew you'd be alright
for the ten mile drive cross-country,
keeping to the back roads.
And Mary, she'd be alright too
now that the lights were out:
her mother had never woken,
the house was calm, and as your feet
crunched on the frosted pebbles
you remembered your musky wetness
on her warm belly
and you began to stir again.
The car was blind,
the windows blank with frost.
You turned the key, expecting
the familiar churn of the starter,
the smell of her still on your fingers
as the detonator whispered
its final goodbyes.

In the Darkroom

I. Preparation

Somewhere I can hear the rustle
of the film as you unroll it,
your breathing in the thick flood.
I'm trying to picture what's been lost:
your pale face above that
mauve jumper, your dark eyes,
the white plastic of the developing reel
as you press it into my hands.
I begin to wind the film
—easy five minutes ago—
but my hands are dumb
in this lightless world,
my senses floundering,
and you have to guide my fingers
with the delicate Braille of your touch.
When you turn on the light
the room leaps back into place,
unabsorbed wavelengths
flooding our retinas.

II. Developing

The mysteries of light caught
on this thin piece of celluloid.
There's an alchemy here
I don't understand, although
you try and explain it to me
as we wait for the chemicals
to reveal what has been hiding,
frozen in darkness.
When you finally show me the film
the ghost of light is there in its opposite,
the world revealed as dark matter,
like those photos of yours,
how you said the ice was black to you:
snow on the river swelling
into the shadowy contours
of a woman's stomach,
the soft grain of her skin.

III. Printing

Weeks later, I watch
as mountains emerge in the printing tray,
glaciers packed between their shoulders,
a dark tide of tree growth
lapping at their flanks.
In the foreground figures are walking
across a white space
which slowly translates itself
into a snowy field, thin wisps of dead grass,
a few footprints. We were at a wedding,
almost anonymous in our hats and scarves.
I remember my fingers, numb
as I held the camera,
the bridegroom trying to play his sax
at twenty below, the bride wrapped
in her parka and smiling.
And you, somewhere among the faces.
I lift the print from the tray—
the acid tang of chemicals
catching in the back of my throat—
lower it into the fixer,
scrutinising the print for your face,
finding it nowhere.

Lazarus

As white as a tuber,
still filthy from the grave,
I stagger back into my life.

The house is shuttered in mourning
and I hide in its dark,
unable to bear the sun's bright lances,
the baying crowds that grow
like a pestilence with each new day.

Their words crash through doors.
What is heaven like?
Will we burn for our sins?
I can tell them nothing:
death was dreamless sleep,
his voice an agony calling me back.

My sisters bring me food,
indecipherable tastes, everything
tainted with the odour of putrefaction.

At night I slip out,
walk the familiar dusty streets.
People I've known since childhood
cross the road to avoid me,
their heads averted.

I see it in my sisters' eyes:
the memory of the opened grave,
something pallid and awful
stirring in the grave-clothes.

In a Japanese Supermarket

This is the land of plenty,
the world's fruits freighted here
in temperature-controlled aircraft,
a cornucopia of kumquats,
bananas and mangoes
bathed in a mist of water-cooled air,
every kind of flesh shrink-wrapped
on Styrofoam trays:
chocolate-pale calves' livers,
blood-wet steaks,
the purple bruise of tuna.
Prawns are packed in layers,
legs and feelers still stirring.
Without impermanence
there can be no beauty
said the Japanese thinker.
And it's there in the boneless ghosts
of dried cod, the steely sardines
like arrow heads,
the scales on the salmon's flank.
See how our eyes have their own hungers,
want to linger over the salmon's sheen,
the slick muscles of sea bass
laid out on ice,
the slippery sacks of nothing
that were once squid.

Eels

Pourings of water,
the river quaking and rucking
as it accelerates over the concrete sluice,
upwellings carrying the stain of its breath.
I climb down to stand at the edge
where water slides,
a sheet of melting glass,
and see eels,
six-inch slivers of darkness,
mouths clamped to the concrete.
Every few seconds one fires upstream,
a writhing cord
thrashing the inch-deep current;
hovers on the rim
before it's flung back,
a loose thread gone in the power surge.
Instinct keeps them coming,
always more, climbing on each other's backs,
catapulting themselves
into the head-on collision of water.
How many make it in an hour?
I counted only one,
large and pale-bellied,
that somehow snaked itself
across a piece of hardly-wet concrete
and was gone,
loosed at the river's head.
Next day most have disappeared,
the few that are left
flagging in the piling current,
thin fuses burning out.

Magpies

There's something prehistoric
about their ratchetings
the hoarse, metallic clatter
two of them are making now
rattling about in that treetop, as if they've just
winged in from the Jurassic
little beefed-up archaeopteryx
sending the other birds spinning away in a panic.
It'll take another million years
to knock the rough edges
off their dinosaur voices
for that machine-gun chatter
to resolve itself into anything like
the long-tailed tit's sibilant fizz
the liquid arpeggios
the blackbird on the lawn
is now pouring out of its small black
rubber-tyre body.

Razor

I watch you shaving your legs in the bath,
the razor grazing the insides of your thigh,
licking its way along the soft folds
on either side of your crotch,
the dark forest of pubic hair stirring
as you raise one calf and then the other.
That razor has rights I no longer have,
to find out your secret places,
to slide down the back of each leg,
your underwater buttocks
so moon-white because
you would never expose them to the sun.
And yet, when you've finished,
when you've sluiced away the soap,
the tiny cut hairs,
it'll be binned and forgotten,
more easily disposed of
than the memories of love.

Quebec

This was the Canada you'd always wanted,
the old fused seamlessly with the new,
like the timber-framed lobby of the quietly
purring hotel, the restaurants serving
moules marinière and endless coffee
but with none of the surly truculence of Paris.

I was fascinated by the St Lawrence,
its cargo of pack-ice that seemed
to swirl around every side of the city,
the knowledge that to the north,
just beyond the few lights on the other bank,
there was whiteness the whole way to the pole.

You'd sprung the trip on me a few days earlier
as a Christmas present, hoping, I guessed,
for something to weave us back together.
At night I lay motionless, listening
to the low hum of the heating,
the huge space of the king-size bed between us,
while outside the lethal floes sped past.

Another Summer

Sussex stifles in the heat,
fields raked by sun,
the panting trees
weighed down with their greenery.

Your uncle points to hangars
that have evaporated like mirages,
runways overrun by battalions of wheat.
He remembers pubs he drank at,

wobbling back through the blackout
on Air-Force issue bicycles
—*it's a miracle no one was killed*—
and flogging Canadian cigarettes

and military blankets smuggled out
under bulky greatcoats.
In the dark of the museum he recognises
a few grainy photographs,

young men leaning nonchalantly on Spitfires,
cigarettes dangling from their lips,
two washing their feet outside a tent
and fighting over the soap.

He can name the ones who died,
slipping from radio contact somewhere over Normandy,
or who, their planes already burning,
crashed short of the runway,

the last fuel erupting in a balloon of flame.
At the gift counter he toys
with a shrapnel paperweight,
telling the woman he was stationed here

and how nothing but the skylines
seem the same.
Outside the light is blinding,
the car a furnace.

We drive away towards Chichester,
its spire still a marker,
although everywhere the trees have grown,
that summer trapped in their rings.

Swifts

Swifts flicker,
a sudden formation overhead,
the indefatigable aerobats
glimpsed for an instant,
each bird trailing a rasping scream
still hitting the walls
seconds into its absence.

The place settles back:
frantic starlings thrashing
luminous wings,
fighting to gain the rooftops,
the Fred-Astaire swallows
capering under the eaves,
crowding the air like insects.

Then a second attack,
a ruddering dash,
the frail furnace of a single bird
blackening into sight,
skimming the house front,
a sprinting mockery
of the other birds' flight.

And the starlings are in a lather,
a hissing fury,
one bird lumbering after the intruder,
hopelessly unwieldy,
the black gymnast already gone,
a high circling speck,
a fine scream thinning to nothing.

Hit and Run

The pheasant lay on the tarmac,
a still cooling meteor
of burnished metals.

Lifting one of its useless wings,
I saw its belly had been torn into:
bright entrails steamed in the sunlight.
A car, I said,

and letting its wing fall,
remembered the panic of the hare
zig-zagging in my headlights,
heard again its bone-wrecking clunk
on the car's underside.

Reverse over it, someone had said,
just to be sure. But I drove on,
appalled at what might still be twitching
back there in the darkness.

Waltz

Somehow his feet remember
as you lead him in a waltz,
your bare feet, his slippers
turning in surefooted circles.

The radio blares and for long
minutes it's possible to believe
he knows who we are, that you're
his third daughter, home from England,

possible to forget how each morning
your mother must school him
in the complex etiquette
of shirt buttons and trouser buckles,

explain what a toothbrush is for
and how it works. Two weeks ago
your sister, alerted by the
hollow music of water on steel,

found him standing over the
oven drawer, urinating
on the gleaming pots, a warm
reek rising to fill the room.

Now you're crooning to him,
Well done, Dad, that's it,
and he seems to be listening,
seems to recognise above

the sing-song slither of the violins,
the last resounding refrain
as the waltz rushes towards its end,
the incantation of love.

The Storm

A month before he died a storm
ripped across the city, lifting cars,
leaving boats stranded on suburban lawns.

Trees he knew as a boy,
huge maples, soaring elms, split
or came toppling down in a roar of branches.

Point Pleasant took the brunt of it:
the park where he'd played hide and seek,
where I'd walk with him sixty years later

as he pointed out the harbour mouth
U-Boats once haunted,
now looked as if it had caught the edge

of a nuclear blast. Up there,
on the top floor of the nursing home
as the big panes flexed,

did he finally resurface, nineteen again,
criss-crossing the Atlantic with war brides,
salt-diesel cramming his lungs,

the south coast of England
about to come over the horizon
for the first time?

Vernon Street

In your sister's dream your father
is skating on Vernon Street,

alive again, the dark
tree-lined road one long rink.

He is alone, carving perfect turns
in the unmarked ice, the hiss

of his skates the only sound.
The houses pass: the one on the corner

where his mother lived;
your sister's old flat; number eleven

where the young widow would
run her hands through his teenage hair.

He knows the dead are in there,
waiting for him,

but for now he still has time
to make use of the old skates,

the leather straps creaking
with each thrust, the thin blades

singing on the ice,
the whole frozen street his own.

Bow River

Here the river is cracked and broken,
its motion stunned into ice,
thick slabs fracturing

where the last moisture
has leaked away into the frozen sand.
Everything in this place speaks of hunger:

skinny pines, their sap slowed
to almost nothing, ransacked pinecones,
a poverty of grass, dead under thin snow,

the fine tattoo of cougar tracks
floating across the ice,
disappearing into the far trees.

Geese

And then there was a white presence
in the garden,
something that could be stoked into a fury,
a hoarse, big-winged beating.

We gave it space, tightening our lives
to allow for what god or demon
had settled in the orchard

now snatching at windfalls
with six snakelike necks.

At other times it could be
silent and grave,
a fleet of small white galleons.

Killing Geese

Gripping the legs, I was almost pulled over
by that brunt acceleration,
                gunning itself,
                        straining for flight;
the neck under a broomstick, my feet on each end,
then a sudden heave
and the windmill of the heart missed.

It made a hole in the day
where the bird had been.

What remained in my hands,
soft, slack and undone,
was cooling machinery.

Expeditions into the flesh
                (the head came off,
                      then entrails slithered out with one hand)
uncovered pipes,
dark, wet passages,
an unseen inside landscape.

Under Cover

Under Cover

It's all she can do not to touch him.
He's driving her home, the streets deserted,
his expression unreadable in the dim
glow. All night she's been troubled
by his presence, his eyes flickering
across the room towards her, the other
guests nothing but an annoying
distraction. Now they've stopped, under cover,
a lay-by out of sight, huge trees looming
over the car. He leans across in the dark
and they kiss, urgent fingers struggling
with shirt buttons, stubborn zips, her bra,
until she can feel his fingers brushing her thighs
and she comes, quickly, gasping with surprise.

Off Guard

Sometimes it catches her unawares,
when she's washing up or putting the kids
to bed, she'll suddenly think of the soft hairs
on the nape of his neck, his lips
when he's talking, the crook of a knee,
his hands on her back bringing her skin alive.
In bed her husband rolls over, absently
runs his fingers along her side,
his cock against her, half-swollen,
and she freezes, hating his wanting,
wishes for dawn, an end to the creeping hours,
for lunchtime and a few minutes stolen
in the back of a car, her life flaring
into being after so many dead years.

Unsinkable

Wife, husband, children all slide away
as the huge ship of their love pulls out,
tickertape streaming down its sides, the quay
shrinking until they can hardly hear the shouts
and cries of well-wishers, the small
explosions shaking the town. They float on,
oblivious to reefs and shoals, the cruel
rocks that lurk just beneath the surface, borne
along on a happiness so vast
they're convinced it must belong to everyone.
Below them, the holed wrecks of the past
subside slowly into memory, rust, bone.
They too were unsinkable, rigged for splendour,
foundered just beyond the harbour.

Away

In another town they sit together
candlelit in Pizza Express, play-acting
at husband and wife, not sure whether
this is a dress rehearsal or the real thing.
After three glasses of wine he has his arm
around her waist, overwhelmed by her perfume.
Back at the B&B they take their time, calm
now where before they rushed to consume
one another in cars, once in a wood
while ramblers scuffed by yards away.
Later, as he pulls out, he sees the torn hood
of the condom, imagines sperm already
chasing down the egg, a child,
the impossibility of it all.

Brighton

Even as they're making love, he wonders
who she is, her wind-tanned face wracked
with pleasure, his body moving inside hers,
their sweat mixing in the overheated
hotel room. Earlier, on the pier,
she'd pushed him up against an empty
hot dog stand, said she didn't care
who saw but that she wanted him, quickly,
right then and there. He'd pulled away,
blethering something about needing
some air. Now in the bathroom mirror
he notices crow's feet tightening
the corners of her eyes, a strand of grey hair,
glimpses his own unfamiliar stare.

Last Letter

In the end he takes the coward's way out,
a letter sent home from Greece with a friend.
I can't do this anymore, I'm burnt out,
I love you, but you must understand,
—she's reading this locked in the downstairs loo—
neither of us has a free hand
the words blur—*there's nothing more I can do.*
She unlocks the door, can hardly stand,
takes the letter, shaking, upstairs,
wishing her husband, the children were gone.
Sobbing as loudly as she dares,
she wraps herself in the eiderdown,
feels her heart thumping in her chest,
a demented machine that will not rest.

Nest

Months later he rings, his voice caressing
her ear, telling her how broken he feels,
how he'd make it work if only he could.
All she can think about is that day, nestling
in the corn, the ticking of her bike's wheels
as it lay hidden next to them, the wood
in the distance soft with the murmurings
of pigeons. He was naked, and leant over,
brushing her stomach with a loose stalk,
running it between her thighs, the glistening
hairs still wet, leaving grains she'd find later
as she slipped her knickers off in the dark.
She'd forgive it all, the withholding, the pain,
just to feel his lips feathering her breasts again.

Hare

The Transit of Venus

In the blue dusk yours is the first light,
acetylene in the southern sky,
eclipsing everything except the moon.
I used to see you as the earth's cool cousin,
your orbit holding hands with ours
as we swung around the sun,
just beyond the reach of its fiery breath.

Now our telescopes watch
as you crawl across the sun's face,
little more than a cinder.
Below clouds of sulphuric acid,
your five hundred degree surface
is blasted by magma, cooking under a greenhouse
of runaway carbon dioxide.

I think of Jupiter, crackling with radiation,
the stone-cold corpse of Pluto,
the thin veil of our atmosphere,
its lie of blue.

Cardiac

for G and L

Before they shocked you back to life
and you found yourself lying
on the operating table again

—an oxygen mask clamped to your face,
the doctor asking a nurse
if you were breathing—

there was nothing, you tell me,
no tunnel with light at the end,
no out-of-body experience,

no bardo state,
just a profound blank
deeper than any sleep.

For those few seconds, you say,
*I died, whatever the medical
profession might want to call it.*

*

Now there's a tramline down your chest,
a pale seam
no amount of sunshine will darken.

I'm marked for life, you say,
...or is it death?
the memory of those moments

when the heart stuttered and stopped
scarred into its tissue.
Sometimes you wake at night,

waiting for the slightest arrhythmia,
a missed beat,
for the thick bagpipe of muscle to falter,

the mindless flesh
thumping in your ribcage.
de dum, de dum, de dum...

Cycle

Is this the body's way of mourning,
the slow tide seeping between your legs,
an egg in there somewhere, smaller than a pinprick?

Whatever assignation was hoped for, it never happened:
my sperm arriving too late or not at all,
the egg's faint hormonal cry lost in a chemical static.

Every month your womb coughs them out,
these unmanned craft, adrift in a sea of blood,
Maydays from the body's dream of resurrection.

IUI

Watching a woman inseminate you,
your feet in stirrups,
her head bowed between your legs
as she works the long catheter through your cervix

I wonder about my part in all this,
the small clear test-tube of washed
and handpicked sperm
she held up a few minutes ago,

my name and date of birth on the side
—*fifty eight million, a great result*—
the close, strip-lit little room
with its magazines and dvds

where I stood that morning, squeezing
a snail trail of semen into the sterilised plastic pot,
my cooling donation collected later
by Linda, the unseen technician.

Afterwards, I hold your hand,
waiting for the spasms in your womb
to subside, then help you dress.
Your arm on my shoulder,

you step into each boot, still a little wobbly,
still needing me by your side
as we walk back down the bright, manless corridor
to the exit and another month.

Natural History

Kingley Vale Nature Centre, West Sussex

These are the casualties,
the ones who never made it
to the tangled safety of the other verge,

their lives seeping away in ditches,
or who, racked with toxins,
lay under bushes, uncomprehending

as a million suns
burned through their bodies.
Now they're pinned and labelled:

a catalogue of flattened rats,
voles and squirrels
frozen in assorted agonies,

the roe faun like a mummified foetus,
its too-long legs
twisted at impossible angles.

An emaciated husk
was once a green woodpecker
that must have died of starvation,

its balding plumage almost colourless.
A pinboard is lined with skulls,
pebble-sized finches and sparrows,

the curlew's beak a huge needle,
four times as long as its head.
And below the skulls, something I can't make out,

a thin dried-up tube of flesh
ending in two big-fingered paws
and a ruff of fur.

A faded card is lying beside it.
Mole, I can still read, *July '69*.
I lift the tube onto my hand.

It weighs almost nothing.
The long claws are like fish bones.
Whatever ate it turned the skin inside out

like a glove, stripping away everything
except this stubborn spine
and these feet with their wrinkled, human palms.

Discovery

We hung offshore,
listening, as if for the first time,
to the sounds of waves

foaming on the beach;
to the inconsolable wail
of unknown seabirds.

We had smelt the land for days,
a faint scent of pine
mingling with the salt breeze:

now it was overwhelming,
the resinous heat a shock
to our starved senses.

As we lowered the boats
and began to pull for shore,
cliffs rose in front of us like ramparts,

the forest hugged its darkness,
an unmitigated growth
crowding out all thoughts of passage.

On the beach we struggled with the boats,
murmured dry-mouthed prayers of thanks,
our words lost in the booming surf.

Bantam

He greets me,
a raucous grating issuing
from his brilliant throat,

the whole feather and bone
frame convulsing
as if trying to choke up

that domineering shout.
The eyes go wide,
the yellowing bony beak gapes,

and it happens again,
this lung-straining yell
splitting the mid-morning calm,

mastering him.
Utterly its instrument,
his small tatty wing beats

clap the air
in ineffectual protest.
Subside.

He settles the glossy ruff
of his neck,
shaking his tiny reptilian head

as if waking from a trance,
begins to pick jerkily
at the ordinary corn I've scattered.

Slug Desire

Blowing through its blowhole,
head down like a bull at a gate,
the slug forges through
forests of grass, over mountainous walls,
streaming a trail of silver in its wake:

a small terrestrial whale
moving through a sea of its own making,

bellowing noiselessly for a mate
in whom to find its moist release.

Afterwards

I catch myself in the mirror,
the familiar topography of my face

altered somehow: the eyes she scrutinised,
the lips that pressed against hers

almost someone else's.
Does it change us a little each time,

this melding of our bodies,
the subtle exchange of DNA?

I remember the first time,
the strangeness of knowing

I'd been inside a woman,
looking down at myself,

the raw part of me
still sluiced in her wetness.

I had given something away:
a wholeness that had finally been broached.

Weasel

This streaming across open ground,
a brown unsteady voltage,
freezing to interrogate the air,
the grass for shit scent.
On a river bank you pry at holes,
rattling the cages of the dumbly domestic,
finding the trace of fear
everywhere.
At night you go baring your needles,
quartering the meadow,
attending to the smallest quiver.
You float over the dew-wet grass,
strike at the soft white throb
of the rabbit's throat
and hold, hold.

Check Up

Every Tuesday you leave,
flanked by two ambulance men
burly as warders, and climb unsteadily
into the closed, antiseptic smell
of the waiting ambulance.

A few hours, and you'll be home again,
left to totter the final yards
up the garden path, your sticks
like two stiff front legs
you haven't yet quite mastered.

You'll nod at the towering foxgloves,
the immaculate borders
the boy now comes to dig, still packed
with the blooms you grew from seed.

And through the half-open door
your wife will watch, as you gape
at the garden you wrestled
to perfection every summer
in a hunched rage.

Birding

That joke about a pair of tits—
we were kissing in the bird hide,
our tongues nesting in each other's mouths.
As my hand cupped your breast,
the door rattled, light flooded the place
and an owl-like old man was blinking at us,
asking hurriedly if we'd seen much activity.

Mussels

In the sink they open slyly,
the occasional shift as one
nudges against another

the only indication that
anything might be alive
inside all that armour plating.

Dropping clacking handfuls
into the already erupting water
where they rattle and bounce

in a burning dance, you argue
they're senseless, deny that
anything so rooted in the plant world

can possibly know pain.
As the tender flesh
melts in our mouths

I remember the limpets
I hacked as a child
from slippery rocks,

their silkiness, how each
creature shrunk back
helplessly into its shell.

Later, as you open to me,
I'm surprised at the pearly
softness between your legs

imagine myself pushing
through something sub-marine
and infinitely vulnerable.

Fresh Paint

She waits now, as every night she waits,
dusk thickening in the trees, the days
drawing in, wondering if he'll be late,
if he'll notice the sunflowers, their rays
fading in the gloom. The cars are coming home,
nudging into their slots, filling up the street.
She remembers their first night here, how they roamed
through the house, astonished at their luck
and as she moves through the darkened rooms
something of that untouched glamour still clings
to the walls, and she longs for the fumes
of fresh paint, their packaged, untried belongings,
the way they christened every room, making love
believing what they had would always be enough.

The Whale

Waterless, it lay under the sky
while the outgoing tide
nibbled at the pebbles
and the loud, airborne gulls
swooped and flocked over
the grey acres of its blubber.
Its breath was another tide
blasting over the stones, becoming
more laboured with every roar.
The small rheumy eye
flickered and waned
and the wilting flukes
stirred the pebbles, thrashing great pits
along either side of its body.
People came to watch its death:
dogs flew across the stones,
then stopped short, nosing the air,
puzzled by what they had thought
was part of the landscape;
a cloud of fishy breath
whipped downwind
and children screamed happily,
running to dodge its clownish shower.
Later, men with ropes arrived,
but by then the tide had left
and was mingling with the horizon.

Coyote

You had broken cover
and now, between the slowing cars
and the wood's beckoning darkness,
on the bowling green verge
you hesitated.
We killed our engine
and sat hushed as
dazzled by sly scents
you nuzzled the air,
a small, bony wolf,
ears pricked and swivelling,
each new sound
stringing you tighter.
Then some car door must have clicked
and as if stung by thrown stones,
you were suddenly running,
glancing back furtively
at the man already standing,
aiming the camera.

Lavant

All winter the river seethed,
a dark tonnage of water
sliding through the city,
could hardly contain itself,
spilled out onto the streets,
quickly gagging the drains,
then boiling up half a mile away.

Nothing, it seemed, could live in that flow,
the underwater avalanche
of stones, branches, abandoned trolleys,
an enormity of water
that could only be tamed
by pumping millions of gallons
away from the fragile culverts the city sat on.

But now this:
rumours of a small translucent smelt
inhabiting the summer waters,
thousands of salt-water ghosts
nosing into the flow, migrating under the city,
emerging into the clear, slow
upper reaches of the reborn river.

Newborn

Her head is too big
for that small, slack neck:
it lolls and bumps, needs holding up.

She is wordless, a fish newly out of water.
My face is a risen moon,
my eyes moving pools of light to her.

Outside it's raining,
a slow tap-tapping giving way
to an insistent pebble-dash on every pane.

Rapt, she is gazing at the streaming glass.

Giant Steps

Now she's upright,
her gait a stumbling run,
as if the world is always

being tipped, a waddling charge
across the unfamiliar lawn
to where her mother's arms wait

to dangle her, a rubbery puppet.
Arrived, safe, she mouths
a squall of excitement,

the word *mama* finding
a first crude shape
on her shapeless tongue.

Alone, she is struggling,
stubby-fingered, starting suddenly
at the zoo of her own voice.

First steps in the
spacesuit of skin, the words
she will grow into.

The Principle of Indeterminacy

And all along, it seems,
it might have been us
that drove the mantis
to consume mate after mate,
their twitching abdomens
still frenzied with pleasure
even as their heads were being torn off.
Scientists now point to a lack of food,
the glare of lights in the laboratory:
half-starved, on the bright stage
of our expectation,
she ate the first thing that moved.
Seen now, for the first time,
her pale, stick-like body and his,
their limbs still trembling,
the fabled act not happened.

The Tranquillity Maps

Their co-ordinates are silence
and the voices of water,

their symbols concealed
in the revelations of bark.

They describe the contours of light,
the seedhead's vocabulary,

mathematics of stillness
and the geography of leaves;

elaborate the progress of lichen,
the wind's unstructured notations.

Hare

for Bethan

Snakes that cast their coats for new
Chameleons that alter hue,
Hares that yearly sexes change.
                    Fletcher: *Faithful Shepherdess*

I

You were surprised by its huge ears,
alert and stiff in the long grass

its masculine nose,
the lithe terrier-like body.

We were almost on it
when the hare erupted into flight

something more like a deer
than a rabbit in the way it ran

bounding in fast surefooted leaps
across the astonished field

until it veered suddenly, rose into the air
and was gone in the dusk of the wood

leaving only this impression
warm in the still unravelling grass.

II

Warm in the still unravelling sheets,
I run my fingers down your spine

trace the soft vestigial hair of an animal
that only minutes ago I held

bucking in my arms, a fierceness
I'd never imagined, straining for release

a changeling that slipped between my fingers
and was gone with a cry

now resolving itself back into you.

Notes

Fast
Verity Linn, a Breatharian, was found dead near a remote Scottish loch in 1999. Breatharians believe that humans can be sustained by prajna alone, the life force that is present in the air, and therefore do not need to eat or possibly even drink

Waltz, The Storm and Vernon Street
These three poems are in memory of H.F. MacLeod (1925-2003)

Lavant
The River Lavant is a seasonal river that runs through Chichester. In November 2000, the river threatened to burst its banks again, as it had done in 1994.

The Principle of Indeterminacy
In quantum physics, Heisenberg's Principle of Indeterminacy states that the position and momentum of particles are impossible to calculate simultaneously, in part because of the effect of the act of observation on the experiment

The Tranquillity Maps
Tranquillity Maps were first produced by the Council for the Protection of Rural England in 1995 to denote the quietest places in the UK. Since that date, subsequent maps have shown a steady decrease in the size and number of quiet places.

Biography

Hugh Dunkerley grew up in Edinburgh and Bath, and now lives in Brighton. He has been a Gregory Award recipient, a Hawthornden Fellow and a Leighton Fellow at The Banff Centre for the Arts. He currently teaches English and Creative Writing at The University of Chichester.